Library of Congress Cataloging-in-Publication Data

Palenque, Stephanie Maher.
    Crack & cocaine=Busted! / Stephanie Maher Palenque.— 1st ed.
      p. cm. — (Busted!)
    Includes bibliographical references and index.
    ISBN 0-7660-2169-6
    1. Cocaine habit—Juvenile literature. 2. Teenagers—Drug use—Juvenile literature.
    I. Title: Crack and cocaine=Busted!. II. Title. III. Series.
    HV5810.P35   2005
    613.8'4—dc22   2004019266

Printed in the United States of America

10 9 8 7 6 5 4 3 2 1

To Our Readers: We have done our best to make sure all Internet Addresses in this book were active and appropriate when we went to press. However, the author and the publisher have no control over and assume no liability for the material available on those Internet sites or on other Web sites they may link to. Any comments or suggestions can be sent by e-mail to comments@enslow.com or to the address on the back cover.

Illustration Credits: Corel Corporation, pp. 28–29, 31, 35, 63; www.dea.gov, pp. 11, 16–17, 21, 54, 69; Digital Stock, pp. 52–53; EyeWire, p. 59; © 2004 JupiterImages, pp. 80, 88; stockbyte, pp. 72–73, 82–83; U.S. Coast Guard, pp. 6–7, 9, 12, 38.

Cover Illustration: U.S. Coast Guard.

Crack & Cocaine=

Stephanie Maher Palenque

Enslow Publishers, Inc.

40 Industrial Road	PO Box 38
Box 398	Aldershot
Berkeley Heights, NJ 07922	Hants GU12 6BP
USA	UK

http://www.enslow.com

*To my parents, Peter and Carole Maher,
who taught me by their example how to
work toward my dreams.*

*And to my wonderful husband, Jaime,
and my three beautiful daughters,
Sophia, Alexandra, and Charlotte, who
have helped me make each one of
my dreams, including the ones I didn't
even know I had, come true.*

*Thank you for your constant support . . .
I love you all.*

CONTENTS

CHAPTER ONE

WILD WEST ON WATER

On May 3, 2001, a 150-foot fishing boat was floating in the eastern Pacific Ocean. But there was no working fishing equipment in sight and hardly any fish on board.

The *Svesda Maru* had moved from international waters, parts of the high seas that are not controlled by any one country, of the Pacific Ocean to about fifteen hundred miles southwest of San Diego.[1] It is part of a 6-million-square-mile area that includes the Caribbean Sea, the Gulf of Mexico, and the eastern Pacific Ocean, called the "Transit Zone."[2] The ship looked like it was heading toward Mexico or Central America. American authorities were watching.

When a U.S. Navy destroyer stopped the *Maru*, they found a crew of eight Ukrainians and two Russians manning the ship. They were taken into custody while the destroyer crew boarded and searched the alleged fishing boat. The Navy searched for five days before the Coast Guard relieved the Navy crew. The search for drugs continued. A U.S. Coast Guard structural engineer took soundings (scientific measurements) of various holes in the *Maru* to locate the drugs they suspected were hidden somewhere on board. About twelve tons of cocaine—approximately twenty-six thousand pounds—was eventually found in the ship's fuel tanks.[3]

The ship was towed to San Diego. News reporters swarmed to photograph the seized cocaine, which was guarded under tight security on the pier. The ship had almost surely been

Sometimes drugs are found in the fuel tanks of ships.

headed toward Mexico or Central America. Its $600 million cargo would most likely have been smuggled overland into the United States and sold on the street to Americans.[4]

During an interview, Randy Harper, a flight engineer, said, "All we knew was that it was a suspect vessel. We didn't know if it had nothing on it, or if it was the motherlode, which it was."[5]

"We're sort of like offensive linemen," said Jim Litz, pilot of the *Svesda Maru* mission. "Our names don't get mentioned in the paper, but we do a lot of the grunt work."[6]

The air above the Mexican–U.S. border is protected by a shield of deterrence in the form of blanket radar coverage. A radar saturation of the border has made would-be smugglers think twice.

This international drug bust of the *Svesda Maru* was the largest at-sea drug bust in history, both in raw size (the amount of cocaine) and in street value (the money the cocaine would make if it was sold).

During the press conferences at the pier where the *Maru* was docked, Coast Guard Pacific Area Commander Vice Admiral Ray Riutta thanked "the brave men and women of many law enforcement agencies."[7]

The drug-smuggling crew of the *Svesda Maru* faces charges of smuggling on the high seas, which could result in life imprisonment. It is likely that their "fishing" days are over. The "good guys" won this battle, but they are painfully aware of the fact that they have not yet won the war.

Among high school students surveyed as part of the 2003 Monitoring the Future Study, 3.6 percent of eighth graders, 5.1 percent of tenth graders, and 7.7 percent of twelfth graders reported using cocaine at least once in their lifetimes.[8]

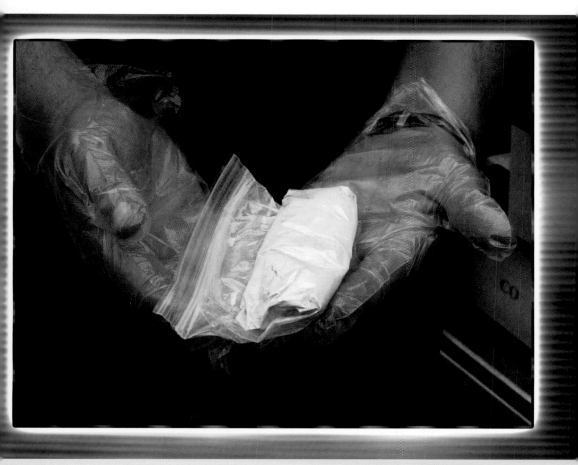

The cocaine found in the *Maru* would have been packaged like this, and in smaller bags, then sold on the street.

Cocaine—over ten thousand pounds—was found on this ship by the U.S. Coast Guard.

The effects of cocaine on our society are far-reaching. The students described above are in danger of being thrown off track from their would-be accomplishments in life. Some might have been Nobel peace prize winners, world leaders, and doctors.

Since September 11, 2001, drug trafficking has been linked with terrorist activities. We now know that these two issues are very much intertwined because drug smuggling can raise money to support terrorism. Although the Drug Enforcement Administration (DEA) does not specifically target terrorists or terrorist organizations, some of the individuals and/or organizations targeted by the DEA may be involved in terrorist activities. In fact, 39 percent of the State Department's current list of thirty-six designated foreign terrorist organizations has some connection with drug activities.

Historically, the DEA has defined narcoterrorism in terms of people like Pablo Escobar, a cocaine trafficker who used terrorist tactics to further his political agenda and to protect his drug trade. Pablo Escobar was a Colombian drug lord who was considered to be one of the most dangerous and powerful drug dealers Colombia

Raphael grew up in Santa Cruz, Bolivia, and remembers the craziness around the drug trade that ensued in the eighties:

> The wealth—and the rapid accumulation of it—was beyond anything you can possibly comprehend. Houses that could be condemned by the health department due to their condition would, all of a sudden, have multiple Mercedes and BMWs pulling up the driveway. A few weeks later, that same house would be demolished to make room for a mansion to be built in its place. During that time, money seemed to be everywhere. Even our carnivals, which are wild to begin with, got more extravagant. The "queens" of the carnivals, and her court, wore dresses that were easily worth $20,000 to $30,000 U.S. dollars.

> We had names for the people who were drug dealers, involved with the cocaine trade—"pichicateros." We even had rhymes we used to recite about them: "Tamaña Bronco vidrios obscuros pichicateros seguro!" The rough translation is, "Look at the size of that Bronco, dark, tinted windows, drug dealers for sure!"[9]

ever had. He made millions of dollars smuggling cocaine into the United States.[10]

During the 1980s, he became known internationally because his drug network, known as *El Cartel de Medellin*, controlled a large portion of the drugs that entered into Mexico, Puerto Rico, the Dominican Republic, Peru, Bolivia, and many other international places mostly through the Americas. It is said that his network might have reached as far as Asia.[11] Today, governments find themselves faced with terrorist groups that participate in or receive money from drug trafficking. Stopping the drug trade has never been more important than it is right now.[12]

CHAPTER TWO

THE LEGEND OF SNOW WHITE

Cocaine comes from the coca leaf, found in South America. While coca does contain cocaine, it does not contain very much. In fact, somewhere between 99.3 and 100 percent of each leaf is not cocaine. However, thousands of years ago, Indian tribes in South America discovered that chewing small amounts of coca over time caused the slow release of natural stimulants. Coca chewers, known as "coqueros," received a slow, constant buzz as they chewed.[1]

These Indians may have known more about the benefits of coca than first thought. A small energy boost is apparently not the only benefit of chewing coca. In June 1974, Tim Plowman, a scientist, decided to get the real story on the dangers (real or imagined) of coca. He sent a kilogram of Bolivian coca leaves for a nutritional breakdown in the United States. The results were surprising. The leaves were so rich in nutrients that he concluded that one hundred grams of the leaf more than satisfied the recommended daily allowance for calcium, iron, phosphorus, and vitamins A, B_2, and E. Fifty-seven grams of coca chewed daily provided the chewer with all the vitamins he needed, which was important since there is a scarcity of fresh fruit and vegetables on the Sierra (the rugged mountain ranges of South America).[2]

Plowman's figures are still contested: Because coca leaves are thrown away instead of swallowed after chewing, it has been pointed out that

Street Names for Cocaine

Cocaine is an alkaloid drug (a drug with a natural nitrogen-containing base) derived from the leaves of the coca shrub. Some of the street names for the drug include:

Coke	Gold Dust
C	Happy Dust
Toot	Icing
Flake	Jelly
Snow	Lady
All-American Drug	Mama Coca
Aspirin	Mojo
Barbs	Nose Stuff
Bernie	Paradise
Big C	Pariba
Candy Sugar	Pearl
Coca	Scorpion
Double Bubble	Sevenup
Florida Snow	Snow White
Foo Foo	Sugar Boogers
Gin	Zip

their nutritional value may not be as high as first reported.

Coca has been used for thousands of years to combat altitude sickness (effects such as nosebleed, nausea, or headache, or oxygen deficiency in the blood and tissues at high altitudes).[3] It was particularly useful in the Andean region of South America for this reason. The Andes Mountains are the longest stretch of mountains in the world. The mountains stretch for 4,500 miles along the west coast of South America. It is also one of the highest mountain ranges in the world.

Altitude sickness does not really have to do with the change in altitude, but with the change in oxygen levels. The higher you go, the less oxygen there is. Coca helps to regulate the metabolism, and is used in the form of coca leaves or *mate de coca* (coca tea) in the Andes region of Bolivia and Peru, where it is perfectly legal. Coca tea contains only a little bit of cocaine. It is not, however, legal in the United States, because the coca leaf (*Erythroylum coca*) is the source of cocaine, a highly-processed derivative of coca. But there is enough to act as a stimulant, which is why Bolivians and Peruvians drink it the same way Americans might enjoy coffee.[4]

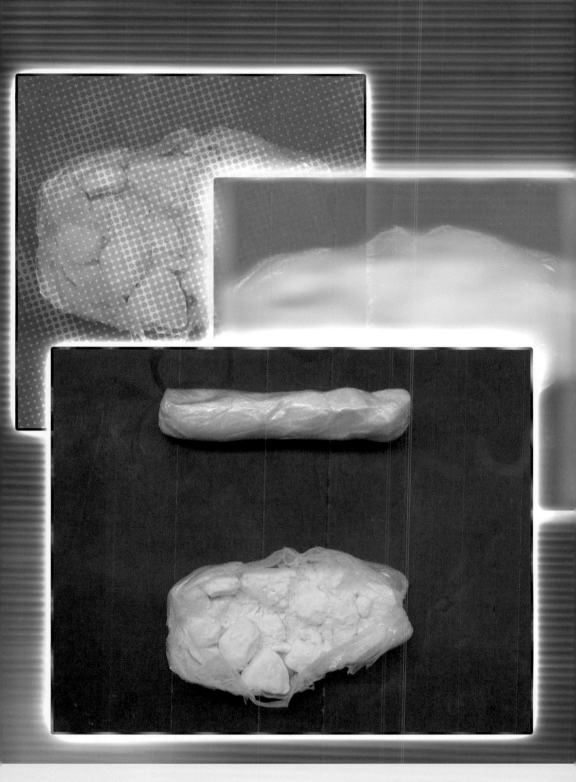

Cocaine is smuggled into the country in small balloons or bags.

MYTH		FACT
You have to use drugs for a long time before they can really hurt you.	vs.	Drugs can cause the brain to send the wrong signals to the body. This can make a person stop breathing, have a heart attack, or go into a coma. This can happen the first time a drug is used.[5]

The coca plant is grown in South America on remote farms located in the Andes Mountains. Most plants will produce leaves for almost fifty years. The leaves of the coca plant are harvested three to four times per year. After the leaves are harvested, they are taken to isolated, secret laboratories located deep in the jungle. Here the leaves are placed into large, in-ground trenches or aboveground vats.

The leaves are treated with salt, covered with gasoline, and allowed to sit. The liquid is later drained and refined into cocaine base. Cocaine base is a pasty substance, which can be smoked. Cocaine base is further refined, using hydrochloric acid, into cocaine HCL or powder cocaine. It takes approximately one hundred fifty pounds of coca leaves to make one pound of powder cocaine.[6]

Cocaine Powder

Cocaine can be snorted, swallowed, injected, or smoked. The street drug comes in the form of a white powder called cocaine hydrochloride. The drug has come to be known as the "drug of choice" for the upper class and celebrities, mostly due to its high price. For such a supposedly "glamorous" drug, the accompanying side effects are decidedly unglamorous: red, bloodshot eyes; runny nose and sniffling; and a change in eating and sleeping patterns. The user may be depressed, withdrawn, and tired. A user may also not care about their appearance and has a frequent need for money.

Just like the coca leaf, cocaine powder had its time and purpose. Doctors and surgeons discovered that cocaine powder is useful in the operating room. Cocaine is used by the medical profession mainly as a surgical anesthetic in eye, ear, nose, and throat surgery, and fiber tube optical examinations of the upper respiratory and digestive tracts. Cocaine has a combination of properties that cannot be duplicated by any of the synthetic local anesthetics. In addition to its anesthetic effect, it constricts small arteries, lessening bleeding.

Other medical uses are rare. Cocaine is an ingredient in Brompton's mixture, a preparation used in Great Britain for treating the chronic pain of terminal cancer. Cocaine powder is still manu-factured legally in the United States. A company that is registered by the federal government is allowed to import coca leaves to the United States. They then extract (draw out) the oil and waxes, which are sold as a flavoring agent. The cocaine paste is then shipped to another federal-ly licensed company, which then manufactures pharmaceutical cocaine from the cocaine base. This is the pharmaceutical cocaine that is used as a local anesthetic.[7]

Substitutes have been found for most therapeutic uses of cocaine, and in most cases its dangers are believed to outweigh its potential benefits. Despite the recent and so-far uncertain signs of reviving interest, coca and cocaine will never again be as widely used in medicine as they once were.[8]

Freebase

Freebase cocaine is cocaine without its water-soluble component or "base." It is prepared by dissolving cocaine hydrochloride with a strong alkali (soluble mineral matter, other than common salt) and drawing out the pure cocaine from many of the impurities. There are extremely explosive solvents involved when preparing freebase cocaine, and it involves much preparation time and equipment. Freebasing originated in the mid-1970s as concern grew about the impurities in cocaine hydrochloride. Because freebase cocaine is not water soluble, it must be vaporized and inhaled to be absorbed. This process is called "smoking," even though it does not involve the actual burning of cocaine.[9]

The smoking of freebase cocaine produces faster and higher peak blood and brain levels of the drug. For this reason, it has caused much alarm and concern. Smoking this form of the drug results in the most rapid delivery to the brain, two to three times faster than the intravenous route. It takes only five to ten seconds for cocaine to reach the brain after inhalation. Clinical studies tell us that addiction is greater and quicker when it is inhaled. Addiction may even happen in weeks, if the drug is smoked.[10]

In the early 1980s, freebase became popular among those searching for the "highest high." Around 1985, the drug dealers wised up and realized that what was being produced was a more potent form of cocaine. The conversion process was time consuming and dangerous and was not suitable for mass production.

Crack

Crack then entered the picture. In the conversion process of crack, the drug is similarly cooked down to a smokeable substance, but the risky

Percentage of Americans Reporting Lifetime Use of Crack, By Age Group, 2002			
Age Group	Lifetime	Past Year	Past Month
12–17	0.7%	0.4%	0.1%
18–25	3.8%	0.9%	0.2%
26 and older	3.9%	0.7%	0.3%
Total Population	3.6%	0.7%	0.2%

Source: National Survey on Drug Use and Health.

process of removing the impurities and hydrochloric acid is taken out, so all that is required is baking soda, water, and a heat source, often from a home oven. Overall, crack delivered "more bang for the buck" by delivering the drug more efficiently. Crack cocaine became available to lower levels of the economic ladder in society. This kicked off the crack epidemic, and social classes from low to high were affected.[11]

Crack is usually smoked from pipes, burnt on a piece of tin foil, or mixed with tobacco and marijuana in a smokeable joint. Crack cocaine, also called "rock," is a form of freebase that comes in small lumps and makes a crackling sound when heated. It is relatively inexpensive, but hits must be repeated often. Crack has made cocaine an equal opportunity drug, one available to those who have less money.

Cocaine has proven to be a difficult drug to combat in the war against drugs because of the dangerous and powerful cartels involved, the international demand for the drug, and the sheer size of the drug's supply. DEA agents continue to fight anyway.

CHAPTER THREE

THE LEGEND OF THE LEAF

Scientists suspect that the original coca was Bolivian, if only from its distribution across the continent of South America. The ordinary little shrub that produces the coca leaf acts like a living chemistry laboratory sucking up nutrients from the dark soil of South America combining them to produce several natural stimulants, one of which becomes an illegal drug.[1]

The drug was highly regarded in the 1880s and 1890s. Pope Leo XII, Sigmund Freud, Jules Verne, and Thomas Edison recommended its use. In fact, Sigmund Freud in his published writing, *On Coca*, recommended cocaine for a variety of illnesses, and for alcohol and morphine addictions. Many of his patients went on to become addicted to cocaine.

Even the popular soft drink Coca-Cola originally contained cocaine.

The Coca Leaf Then

But let us start from the beginning . . . the very beginning. Coca plant leaves were picked and chewed by the Indians of Peru and other South American countries. Because this practice began before recorded history, our understanding of its start is limited to what archaeologists tell us about it. Archaeologists have learned from line drawings on pottery found in northwestern South America that coca chewing was a large part of the culture before the rise of the Inca Empire.

The Inca Empire was the greatest and best-organized empire in the Americas. The name Inca

The Incas created terraces on the mountainside to make farming easier.

was originally the title of the emperor, who claimed to be the child of the sun. But over time, the name Inca came to mean all the people living in the empire.

The empire prospered. Inca rulers made sure that everyone had enough to eat. Each farmer was given enough land to meet his family's needs. But farmers were allowed to keep only one third of their crops. Another third went to the Inca

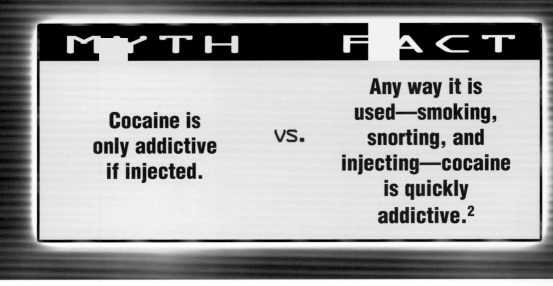

MYTH		FACT
Cocaine is only addictive if injected.	vs.	Any way it is used—smoking, snorting, and injecting—cocaine is quickly addictive.[2]

priests. The final third went to the Inca emperor, to be put in a storehouse to feed the army, government officials, and any people unable to feed themselves. In times of famine, the storehouses saved the people from starvation.

The life of the common people was hard. The steep mountains, poor soil, and dry coastal land made growing enough food difficult. But with the help of skilled architects, engineers, and stonemasons, the Inca found solutions to all of these problems.

On steep mountainsides, they carved out planting areas called terraces that looked like stair steps. In coastal areas, where it seldom rained, farmers built canals to bring water down from the mountains to irrigate their crops.

The Inca Empire provided for almost every need of the people, but gave them little freedom or privacy. Homes could not have doors so that they could be inspected for cleanliness. Inca officials even told young people whom to marry.

The empire was in many ways as advanced as any civilization in Europe, even though it did not have a written language. The capital city of Cuzco was "so beautiful and has such fine buildings," wrote one observer. "It would be remarkable even in Spain."[3]

Though, the Inca did have something that Europeans did not have—an incredible wealth of gold and silver. When they reached the newly discovered lands in 1525, Spanish explorers heard of the Inca's wealth and set out to get it at all costs.

The Inca emperor died right before the Spanish arrived. Two of his sons fought a bloody war to decide who would rule. One son killed the other, and then the Spanish captured and killed the victor.

The Inca Empire was destroyed within six years by the Spanish. Millions of Inca people died, not just in battle, but also from disease, such as smallpox, that the Spanish brought from Europe. Those who survived became poor and powerless.

The Spanish tried to wipe out all traces of Inca

culture. Yet today, some of the Inca ways of life survive. In the highlands of Peru, buildings are still built of stone and adobe, just as they were during Inca days. Farmers still grow crops on terraced mountainsides, and Peruvian villagers still hold markets on ancient Inca sites.[4]

The coca plant was considered to be a gift from the gods and was used during religious rituals, burials, and other special occasions. By the time the Spaniards arrived in the sixteenth century, coca was being used both by members of the ruling class and Indians who worked in the fields. At first, the Spaniards believed that coca use was a barrier to the Indians' conversion to Christianity, so they tried to stop the Indians from using coca.

Later, it became common practice to pay the Indians in coca leaves in exchange for their work. This way, the Spaniards could force enormous amounts of work from them in the gold and silver mines despite difficult conditions in the high altitudes. The Indians were able to fight off fatigue by chewing on the unprocessed leaves for their stimulating effect. Even today, the natives of the Andes still mix the leaves with ashes or lime. They can work for days without feeling hunger or

Quote on Cocaine

"I was sitting, handcuffed, in the back of a police car. Earlier that night, I smashed my car while driving high on coke. My parents had called the cops on me. The police actually came into my bedroom and took me away wearing only shorts and a T-shirt. I was barefoot. As the car backed out of our driveway, I watched my mom crying hysterically. But even more disturbing, was my father. He just stood there staring at me. I stared back in total disbelief. I felt betrayed. I spent the whole night in jail, awake, angry, uncomfortable, shocked, freaked out. How could my family do this to me? But now, three months into treatment, I feel grateful. I was out of control. I could have killed someone. Or myself."[5]

fatigue. But there are side effects associated with repeated chewing of coca leaves. These side effects include an unsteady gait, green-crusted teeth, insomnia, and general apathy.

In the sixteenth century, coca leaves, along with coffee, tea, and tobacco, were brought to Europe from South America by explorers. Unlike the other products, coca leaves were not popular until the nineteenth century. This was probably because coca leaves deteriorated on the way to the final destination. During the long trip, the potency of the leaves was compromised.

Coca use really took off in the Western Hemisphere when it was blended with an alcoholic beverage. Vin Mariani was a coca wine that was launched in 1863. It contained six milligrams of cocaine per ounce of wine. Coca wine was developed by the Corsican entrepreneur, Angelo Mariani (1838–1914). Mariani first tried his new tonic on a depressed actress, and the results were spectacular. Soon after that, she told all of her friends. Mariani wrote a book eulogizing coca. His coca wine made him famous, especially among writers such as Anatole France, Henrik Ibsen, Émile Zola, Jules Verne, Alexander Dumas, Robert Louis Stevenson, and Sir Arthur Conan

Doyle; composers Jules Massenet, Charles Gounod, and Gabrieal Fauré; and royalty as well: Queen Victoria, King George I of Greece, King Alphonse XIII of Spain, and even William McKinley, president of the United States. Religious leaders transcending different religions also used Vin Mariani.

The Coca Leaf Now

Coca leaf production continues even today. As recently as September 2004, coca growers protested against the Peruvian government's attempts to deter the crop's production.

Coca producers who wanted the government to buy more of their crops of coca leaves marched toward Machu Picchu. They had walked all night, more than twenty-two miles, to one of Peru's most popular tourist destinations.

Mayor Oscar Valencia of the tourist town Aguas Calientes turned back the one hundred seventy coca growers with food and a bit of friendly advice. Valencia told the coca growers that if they tried to occupy Machu Picchu, it would violate a sacred sanctuary and would anger the apus, or mountain gods. After all was said and done, the mayor offered the protesters

The U.S. Coast Guard plays a big part in stopping illegal drugs from getting into the United States.

a free train ride home, which they gratefully accepted.[6]

Peruvian coca growers often protest attempts to discourage the production of coca crops. They say that coca leaves are part of Andean culture and have been used for centuries in ceremonies or chewed to ward off hunger. The government claims that the vast majority of the coca is used to produce cocaine.

Peru's government allows the growing of about twenty-five thousand acres of the plant for chewing and for sale to companies that produce pharmaceutical cocaine, package coca tea, or make extracts used in soft drinks. According to Julio Cordero, the regional head of ENACO, the state-run agency that buys legal coca, the government planned to buy 2.9 tons of the leaf in 2004, about the same amount as they purchased in 2003, but Peruvian growers wanted to sell 4 tons.[7]

Doctors started to use cocaine as a local anesthetic for eye surgery in 1884. Cocaine fulfilled all of the requirements of the "ideal anesthetic"—a drug that would effectively and reversibly block the pain impulses sent to the brain and keep the patient fully conscious without the dangers of chemical sleep. The benefits of cocaine as an anesthetic were important in the history of surgery. Coca leaves and cocaine rose to the pinnacle of pharmacology and medicine. The anesthetic properties of cocaine were used for making medications against birth pains, ointments for hemorrhoids, solutions to relieve teething pains in infants, and drops for earaches, in addition to the numerous applications in all surgical cases of various medical specialties.

In 1886, Coca-Cola was first introduced by John Pemberton. It contained cocaine-laced syrup and caffeine. Until the early 1900s, a typical serving of Coca Cola contained around sixty milligrams of cocaine. It was advertised as "The drink that relieves exhaustion." It still relieves exhaustion, but now it does not depend on cocaine to do it. The company replaced the cocaine with caffeine in 1901.

Coca Cola still contains an extract of coca leaves. The Coca Cola Company exports about eight tons of coca leaves from South America each year. Today, the leaves are used only for flavoring since the drug has been removed.[8]

People soon began to realize the negative effects of cocaine. People started to snort cocaine, leading to the first cases of nasal damage from snorting cocaine reported in medical literature. The lining of the nose is damaged, and the septum can be eaten away by cocaine. Cocaine users started to show up in hospital emergency rooms with cocaine-related nasal injuries. In 1912, the United States reported a staggering five thousand cocaine-related deaths.

The Ban on Cocaine and the Harrison Narcotics Act

Cocaine was banned in the United States in 1914 under the Harrison Narcotics Act. Originally, it was meant to be a registration law: doctors, pharmacists, and vendors would submit paperwork on all drug transactions. But the government quickly used violations of the law to shut down legitimate practices as well as illegal drugstores. Restricting the legitimate practice of medicine was not the original intention of the Harrison Act. Thousands of physicians, pharmacists, and addicts were arrested.[9]

In 1918, after three years of the Harrison Act and its devastating effects, a committee was appointed to look into the problem. The chairman of the committee was Congressman Homer T. Rainey. This was the first of a long line of such committees. Among the committees findings were:

- Opium and other narcotic drugs, including cocaine, were being used by about a million people.
- The underground traffic in narcotic drugs was about equal to the legitimate medical traffic.
- The wrongful use of narcotic drugs had increased since passage of the Harrison Act. Twenty cities, including New York and San Francisco, had reported such increases.[10]

As a result of these findings, the committee called for stronger law enforcement and more laws modeled after the Harrison Act. Congress responded by tightening up the Harrison Act. An article in the *Illinois Medical Journal* in June 1926 concluded:

> "The Harrison Narcotic Law should never have been placed upon the Statute books of the United States. It is to be granted that the well-meaning blunderers who put it in there had in mind only the idea of making it impossible for addicts to secure their supply of 'dope' and to prevent unprincipled people from making fortunes and fattening upon the infirmities of their fellow men."[11]

But that is by no means the end of the story. In a way, it was just the beginning. Cocaine now falls under Schedule II of the Controlled Substances Act. The Controlled Substances Act (CSA), Title II of the Comprehensive Drug Abuse Prevention and Control Act of 1970, is the legal foundation of the government's fight against the abuse of drugs and other substances. This law is a consolidation of numerous laws regulating the manufacture and distribution of many types of drugs as well as the chemicals used in the illicit production of controlled substances.

The CSA places all substances that are regulated under existing federal law into one of five schedules. This placement is based upon the substance's medicinal value, harmfulness, and potential for abuse or addiction. Schedule I is reserved for the most dangerous drugs that have no recognized medicinal value, while Schedule V is the classification used for the least dangerous drugs. The act also provides a tool for substances to be controlled, added to a schedule, decontrolled, removed from control, rescheduled, or transferred from one schedule to another.

Cocaine continues to grow in popularity, and

with that, so does the cost. In the early 1930s, Japan was the world's leading producer of cocaine producing 23.3 percent, followed by the United States, Germany, the United Kingdom, and France. By 1981, wholesale cost of one kilogram of cocaine was $55,000.

Freebase

Freebase, a new form of cocaine, was developed in the 1970s. Freebase is cocaine without its water-soluble content, or "base." It is prepared by dissolving cocaine hydrochloride with a strong alkali and drawing out the cocaine from many of the impurities. Preparing freebase cocaine involves highly explosive solvents and requires significant preparation time and equipment.

Freebasing originated at a time when many people were concerned about the impurities found in cocaine hydrochloride. Because freebase cocaine is not water-soluble, it must be vaporized and inhaled to be absorbed.

Drug use was a major social problem of the 1980s. Drug use, abuse, and misuse emerged into the limelight as perhaps never before. It is possible that in no other decade has the issue of drugs occupied such a huge and troubling space in the public consciousness. And it is possible that no specific drug has dominated center stage the way that cocaine and crack did in the 1980s.

In the 1980s, Nancy Reagan, first lady during the Reagan Administration, began her "Just Say No" campaign. The campaign was well known and highly publicized, but it was not nearly enough to stop the use and abuse of cocaine.

Cocaine and Politics

Drug policy has been a part of the political world for decades—used as a playing piece in the game of power, in different ways, for years.

Many Americans have seen the now-famous picture of President Richard M. Nixon shaking the hand of American icon Elvis Presley in the Oval Office after naming him a "federal agent-at-large" for the Bureau of Narcotics and Dangerous Drugs on December 21, 1970. The picture is famous because we now know that Presley, even at the time the picture was taken, was a serious drug addict.[12] Presley was found dead in his bathroom on August 16, 1977, from congestive heart failure. A later autopsy revealed that drug abuse might have been a contributing factor.

In the 1980s, when drug use was a major problem, First Lady Nancy Reagan started a public crusade against the dangers of drug and alcohol use and abuse. She went to sixty-five cities in thirty-three states, the Vatican in Italy, and eight other foreign countries over eight years. She made many speeches and hosted two international conferences. In an interview with *Good Morning America* in November 1981, Reagan said her "best role is to try to bring public awareness, particularly parental awareness, to the problems of drug abuse" because "understanding what drugs can do to your children, understanding peer pressure and understanding why they turn to drugs is . . . the first step in solving the problem."[13]

Reagan's campaign was called "Just Say No," and until then, there had never been a higher-profiled government antidrug program. It was a noble and ambitious act on Mrs. Reagan's part but the campaign slogan "Just Say No" did not work as hoped. Studies indicate that it did not keep kids away from drugs at all. Drug use among teenagers dropped steadily from the early eighties until 1992, mirroring a decline in drug use among adults. But this downward trend began before the antidrug program developed in the 1980s could have had any impact. The drop was detected in surveys of students who had never heard of "Just Say No."[14]

The Clinton administration took a much more subtle approach to the war against drugs. In late 1997, Congress created an enormous financial reward—as much as $25 million for the following year-and-a-half—for television executives to push antidrug messages in the stories of television shows, including *ER*, *Beverly Hills 90210*, *The Drew Carey Show*, and *7th Heaven*.[15]

The White House Office of National Drug Control Policy gave up the advertising time in return for getting antidrug messages included in specific primetime shows. This created a new antidrug campaign run by the government, and it allowed the networks to resell their airtime to companies willing to pay top dollar for it.

It seemed like a good idea, but some argued that the arrangement may have violated laws that require networks to report, during a show's broadcast, arrangements with any party providing financial considerations, however direct or indirect.[16]

The DEA

The real heroes in the war against drugs are the Drug Enforcement Administration agents.

As the government's role in the control and restriction of drugs has increased, so has the involvement of various federal agencies. But no agency has more direct involvement with illegal drugs than the DEA, whose headquarters is located in Washington, D.C.

Prior to the creation of the DEA, the two agencies charged with drug law enforcement were the Bureau of Drug Abuse Control (BDAC) and the Federal Bureau of Narcotics (FBN). The agencies were effective, but duties were overlapped and confusing. President Richard M. Nixon combined the existing agencies to form the DEA on July 1, 1973. The mission of the DEA is to

enforce the controlled substances laws and regulations of the United States and bring to the criminal and civil justice system of the United States . . . those organizations . . . involved in the growing, manufacture, or distribution of controlled substances . . . destined for illicit traffic in the United States; and to recommend and support non-enforcement programs aimed at reducing the availability of illicit controlled substances on the domestic and international markets."[17]

The United States had a full-blown war on their hands, and the DEA was the military. The drug of the 1980s was cocaine, so that had to be the target. The DEA decided to wage an attack on cocaine where it starts—production. The coca leaf is grown throughout most of South America, but mostly in Bolivia, where there are labs that convert the coca leaf to base.

In July 1986, the DEA launched Operation Blast Furnace. The DEA and the Bolivian Narcotics Strike Force troops launched raids against cocaine laboratories in Bolivia. Before the raids, DEA intelligence analysts had been sent to Bolivia where they helped identify several major Bolivian violators.[18]

Black Hawk helicopters transported the strike teams to the suspected laboratory sites. Eight cocaine laboratories and one shipment location were located and destroyed. Some of the labs destroyed had been capable of producing one thousand kilograms of cocaine per week. At least one lab had been in operation since 1982.[19]

Operation Blast Furnace brought cocaine production to a virtual standstill in Bolivia.

Raphael grew up in Santa Cruz, Bolivia, and remembers the craziness around the drug trade that ensued in the eighties:

I remember the Black Hawk helicopters from the United States flying overhead. They were traveling in a group when I saw them. We knew exactly where they were from, because they were so high-tech. Doors were open, and men in full military garb where standing at the doorway, poised to shoot. The next morning, I read in the newspapers about how many people were killed in the battle.

After that, the money disappeared, slowly, but surely. Crime, especially in Santa Cruz, increased. People were desperate to make a living. Until that time, the drug trade carried everything, and most products we used on a daily basis were imported. With no more production, and no money to import, everything dried up.[20]

Traffickers fled the country and coca paste buyers from Colombia stayed away. Following the success of Operation Blast Furnace, the DEA and other agencies were able to follow up with other operations to end coca growth and cocaine production.[21]

According to the Drug Enforcement Administration, they now employ more than 9,000 employees with more than 4,500 special agents located in communities across the United States and around the world. In order to meet the challenges posed by sophisticated international drug trafficking organizations, the DEA has developed state-of-the-art investigative tools and techniques that are used in twenty-two field divisions, offices in more than fifty foreign countries, and in high-tech laboratories around the nation.

The DEA does not work alone. It works together with members of the international community in targeting the highest levels of drug mafias around the world. Drugs are not just a problem in the United States, but all around the globe.

CHAPTER FOUR

THE PRICE TO PLAY

Cocaine is a highly addictive drug. It is very easy to go from just trying the drug to being an addict. Some experts say that cocaine is so powerful that the onset of addiction occurs on the user's first try. When tested on animals, cocaine causes animals to go to great lengths (press a bar more than ten

Crack, seen here, and cocaine are both highly addictive drugs.

thousand times) to get just one "hit," choosing cocaine over food and water, and taking cocaine even when this behavior is punished by electric shock. The animals must have their access to cocaine limited in order not to take toxic or even lethal doses.[1]

People addicted to cocaine behave similarly to the animals that choose cocaine over food and water. They will go to great lengths to get cocaine and continue to take it even when it hurts their school or job performance and their relationships with loved ones.

In order to understand why someone would let cocaine take over his or her entire life, there must be a good understanding of the physical effects that cocaine has on the body. The effects of cocaine are immediate and extremely pleasurable for most, but brief. Cocaine and crack cocaine both produce intense but short-lived euphoria, a feeling of great happiness or well-being, and can make users feel more energetic. Cocaine produces wakefulness and reduces hunger.

Psychological effects include feelings of well-being and a grandiose sense of power and ability mixed with anxiety and restlessness. As the drug wears off, these feelings are replaced by an intense depression, and the drug user will then crash, becoming lethargic and typically sleeping for several days.[2]

When examining cocaine addiction, the pleasurable effects of the drug must also be examined. Scientists have discovered regions within the brain that, when stimulated, produce feelings of pleasure. One neural system that appears to be the most affected by cocaine originates deep within the brain. Nerve cells originating in this area extend to an area of the brain known as a key pleasure center. In studies using animals, for example, all types of pleasurable stimuli, such as food, water, sex, and drugs of abuse, cause increased activity in this pleasure center.

Researchers have discovered that cocaine use interferes with the normal communication process that happens within the brain. The result is the feeling commonly described as euphoria by many cocaine users.

The duration of cocaine's immediate euphoric effects depends on how the drug was taken. The faster the absorption, the shorter the duration of action. The high from snorting is relatively slow in onset and may last fifteen to thirty minutes, while that from smoking may last five to ten minutes. The short-term physiological effects of cocaine include constricted blood vessels, dilated pupils, and, increased temperature, heart rate, and blood pressure. Large amounts intensify the user's high but may also lead to bizarre, erratic, and violent behavior. These users may experience tremors, vertigo, muscle twitches, or paranoia. Or with repeated doses, users could experience a toxic reaction closely resembling amphetamine poisoning, which is a toxic state following amphetamine use, which can be fatal.[3] Symptoms include high blood pressure, rapid heart rate, agitation, increased body temperature, stroke, seizures, cardiac arrhythmia, coma, and death.

As cocaine abuse continues, tolerance often develops. This means that higher doses and more frequent use of cocaine are required for the brain to register the same level of pleasure experienced during initial use. Cocaine has been found to cause the body to eliminate some of the receptors in the pleasure centers. This causes some destroying of the sensory mechanisms, which causes users to need more and more of the drug to get high. Over time, it ruins their own chances

Cool Ways to "Just Say No"

1. Avoid situations altogether where you know you will be put in a tough situation. If you are invited to a party where you know or think drugs may be used, plan to do something with your real friends (those who share your interests) instead. If you are at a party where drugs are offered to you unexpectedly, speak your mind. Saying something like "I thought I was at a cool party . . . everyone knows that drugs are not cool."

2. If someone approaches you at school and tries to interest you in buying or trying drugs, tell them that you respect your body and love being healthy and drugs do not fit into your plan. Who wants to feel sick and out of control?

3. Get excited about where you are heading. Pick an interest of yours and become an expert on it. You would be surprised how much respect and admiration you acquire when you become "known" for something special at your school. You may even make a few additional friends who share your interests.

4. Do volunteer work. You will be helping others, and feel great about yourself while you are doing it.

5. "Coolness" is all in your attitude. Act as if where you are is "the place to be" and what you are doing is "the thing to do." If you lead the pack and make it clear that you think drugs are not cool, others will surely follow your lead.

of experiencing pleasure from anything else. During periods of abstinence from cocaine use, the memory of the euphoria associated with cocaine use, or mere exposure to cues associated with drug use, can trigger tremendous craving and relapse to drug use.

Physical consequences of cocaine use include increased heart rate, muscle spasms, convulsions, and permanent damage to nasal tissue. Seizures, strokes, respiratory failure, and heart attacks can lead to fatality. First-time users are not excluded from fatal consequences. Cocaine use has been linked to many types of heart disease. Cocaine has been found to trigger chaotic heart rhythms, called ventricular fibrillation, accelerate heartbeat and breathing, and increase body temperature and blood pressure, which can lead to bleeding in the brain.

Different routes of cocaine administration can produce different adverse effects. Snorting cocaine

"My friends think drugs are useless. They ruin your body and you never know how you are going to react and how fast you are going to react to the drug."[4]

can lead to loss of sense of smell, nosebleeds, problems with swallowing, hoarseness, and an overall irritation of the nasal septum, which can lead to a chronically inflamed, runny nose. Ingested cocaine can cause severe bowel gangrene due to reduced blood flow. People who inject cocaine have puncture marks, called tracks, most commonly in their forearms. Intravenous cocaine users may also experience an allergic reaction, either to the drug or to additives often found in street cocaine, which can result in death. Because cocaine users lose their appetite as a side effect of the drug, they can experience significant weight loss and malnourishment.

Although long-term users may feel like they have some kind of control over their usage because they feel as though they know their body's reaction to the drug, they actually have very little control. A tolerance to the drug often develops over long-term use, so that the user needs more and more of the drug to produce the same effect. But sometimes the opposite happens—they may become more sensitive to cocaine's anesthetic effects without ever increasing the amount of usage.

Cocaine and Other Drugs in Hollywood

Where there is fame, money, and power, there will be cocaine and other hard-hitting drugs.

Unfortunately, the combination of celebrities and drugs is nothing new in Hollywood. Many stars have used drugs, and some today are still battling their addictions. Other stars have lost the battle and their lives.

"I've seen all sorts of things," says producer Aaron Spelling. "Young people have more access to drugs. They can ruin lives so quickly."[5]

"The more youthful celebrities who are handed all this wealth and power are giving themselves high expectations at an age before they are mature enough to deal with doing fabulously well," says Stuart Altschuler, a psychotherapist who works with young stars.[6]

As a celebrity, access to illegal drugs is increased. Drugs can be found on many movie and television sets and in other places young Hollywood gathers.

"There isn't a club in Hollywood that doesn't have some sort of a drug problem," says Los

As in many cities, drugs are a problem in Hollywood.

Angeles Police Department (LAPD) Narcotics lieutenant Bernie Larralde.[7]

"The drugs out there today are stronger and more deadly," says Larralde. "The marijuana is more potent, the cocaine isn't cut as much and the heroin is stronger. What's more, you can sniff heroin now instead of injecting it, so you won't have marks on your arm, and you can smoke cocaine in a cigarette—and it's more potent than rock cocaine."[8]

Dr. Mark Goulston, a psychiatrist at UCLA who has treated many big industry names, says typical celebrity addicts think they can control the drug use "just to get through filming a movie or just to help them get some sleep."[9]

That is when things are going well. What follows are three stories of celebrities who reached for the stars—and tripped along the way.

David Strickland (actor; he played Todd Stites on *Suddenly Susan*)

David Strickland was a manic-depressive who was self-medicating with cocaine and alcohol. He appeared to have been in a period of rapid cycling, feelings of intense highs and lows right after each other. The drugs he did magnified the situation.

In his final moments, he lined up all of the beer bottles he had drank, put his pager and wallet next to the bottles, hopped up onto a chair, tied a bed sheet around his neck, with the other end tied to a beam near the ceiling, and kicked away the chair.[10]

River Phoenix (actor; his movies included *Stand by Me* and *The Mosquito Coast*)

River Phoenix was born in a log cabin in Oregon in 1970. His family was very poor. It was only after Phoenix appeared in the movie *Stand by Me* that his family was able to buy a new car.

He and his family were all vegetarians. He believed that eating animals was wrong. As a child, Phoenix convinced his family to become vegetarians. His opinions on the issue were so strong that when his actress girlfriend, Martha Plimpton, ordered soft-shell crab at a restaurant, he was reported to have begun to cry in disappointment.[11]

In the early morning hours of October 31, 1993, River Phoenix was convulsing on a sidewalk. The seizure led to his death. The 911 call was played on many entertainment magazine shows through the weekend and into the following week. Those who did not witness the scene listened to the painful, frantic phone call from a well-known television actress begging for help.

He died at the age of twenty-three of a cocaine and heroin overdose. He was cremated, and his ashes were scattered over the family ranch in Florida.[12]

Chris Farley (actor, comedian, cast member of *Saturday Night Live*, 1991–1995)

Chris Farley's dream came true when he was

chosen to be a cast member of *Saturday Night Live* (SNL), the former employer of a comedian he idolized, John Belushi. John Belushi was a cast member of SNL from 1975 to 1979. He was found dead at the age of thirty-three on March 5, 1982. The cause of death was a lethal injection of cocaine and heroin—a "speedball." Chris Farley would follow in Belushi's footsteps in more ways than one.

Farley was one of SNL's most popular cast members during the 1991 to 1995 seasons. He went on to star in a number of movies with former fellow SNL cast member, David Spade, including *Tommy Boy* and *Black Sheep*.

Farley was in many ways a contradictory character. He was completely uninhibited onstage and in front of the camera and was known to do anything for a laugh, but he could be very shy and insecure in private.[13]

Farley struggled with his obesity, alcohol, and drug addiction for many years, and was found dead in his Chicago apartment on December 18, 1997. An autopsy revealed that Farley had died of an accidental overdose of cocaine and heroin.[14]

Percentage of Students Reporting Crack Use, 2001–2002

Grade	Lifetime		Past Year		Past Month	
	2001	2002	2001	2002	2001	2002
8th Grade	3.0%	2.5%	1.7%	1.6%	0.8%	0.8%
10th Grade	3.1%	3.6%	1.8%	2.3%	0.7%	1.0%
12th Grade	3.7%	3.8%	2.1%	2.3%	1.1%	1.2%

Source: Monitoring the Future Study.

Crack

Crack causes a more intense high, so it is considered to be more highly and more quickly addictive than snorted cocaine. It causes a very abrupt increase in heart rate and blood pressure, which can lead to a heart attack and stroke even in people with no history of vascular disease, and sometimes the first time the drug is used.

Users mainly smoke crack cocaine. However, researchers have found that crack is also sometimes injected or snorted. In some cities, crack cocaine is combined with other substances and injected. For example, in Washington D.C., it was reported that crack is combined with heroin and marijuana and then injected. In New Orleans, Louisiana, it was reported that crack was injected with heroin. Crack was also sprinkled in cigarettes and smoked. These cocaine and crack-cocaine-laced joints are referred to as "primos."[15]

When users mix cocaine and alcohol, they are magnifying the danger of each drug. They unknowingly form a complex chemical experiment within their bodies. Researchers have found when the human liver combines cocaine and alcohol it manufactures a third substance, cocaethylene, which intensifies cocaine's effects. This combination increases the risk of sudden death.

Sudden death takes place when the user's body chemistry just is slightly imbalanced. Toxic chemicals are released into the body creating a reaction resulting in cardiac arrest. This negative reaction to crack cocaine's toxic chemicals is the cause of sudden death.[16]

Crack also crosses the placental barrier. Babies born to crack-addicted mothers go through withdrawal because they are usually born already addicted to crack, and are at a higher risk of stroke, cerebral palsy, and other birth defects.

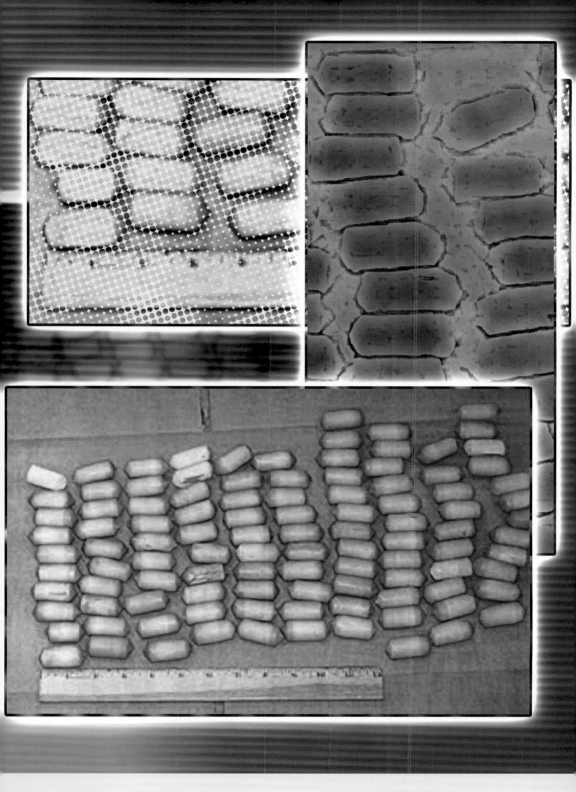

In order to smuggle cocaine and other drugs into the United States, people may place small amounts of cocaine into balloons. They then swallow the balloons.

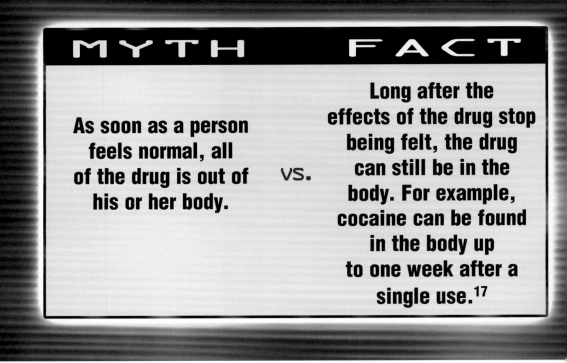

MYTH		FACT
As soon as a person feels normal, all of the drug is out of his or her body.	vs.	Long after the effects of the drug stop being felt, the drug can still be in the body. For example, cocaine can be found in the body up to one week after a single use.[17]

If babies are exposed in the first few months of pregnancy, they can have serious damage to the part of the brain that controls decision-making, judgment, and self-control. The babies quickly came to be known as "crack babies."

Body Packer Syndrome

According to Captain David Campbell of the Investigations Section at the Los Angeles County Department of the Coroner, not only does his department see cocaine deaths as a result of personal use, but also sees them as a result of smuggling cocaine by ingestion—swallowing balloons or plastic bags full of the drug.[18]

Victims of the "Body Packer Syndrome," as it

is sometimes referred to, have been found dead in hotel rooms with little or no drug paraphernalia at the scene. However, laxatives and enema kits were present. Some carriers have died aboard airplanes. Witnesses have reported seeing these carriers behaving in an agitated manner, ending with seizures, respiratory collapse, and death.

Several victims have gone to emergency rooms with symptoms such as mydriasis (prolonged dilation of the pupil of the eye), seizures, and coma. In cases such as these, balloons, condoms, or plastic bags were filled with the drug and swallowed or inserted into the rectum or vagina. Because these bags are semipermeable, they do not have to break in order to cause problems.[19] The cocaine can seep through the bags into the carrier's body.

Many of these users supposedly had it all figured out—the effects of the drug (or combination of drugs) they were using, how they planned on hiding the drugs they possessed from police officers, agents, or doctors. Then, something went horribly wrong. Life is never completely predictable, and it is totally unpredictable when you are using illegal drugs. That is just the price they pay to play.

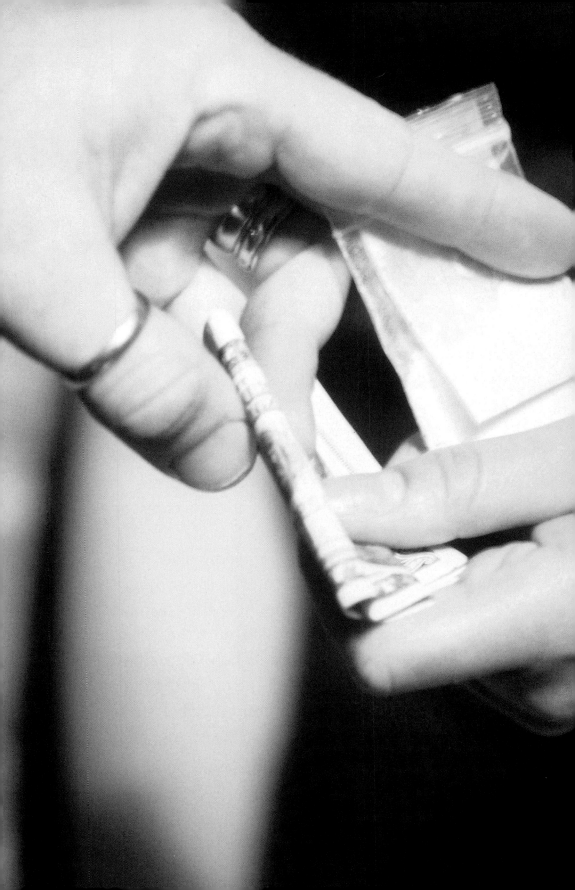

CHAPTER FIVE

TIME TO FACE THE MUSIC

The sexy, rhythmic sounds of Miles's prized black, razor-shaped guitar traveled through the smoke-filled club. The bar was filled with drunken people partying the night away, as it was every night.

Miles was there, as he was every other night—this is the world he lived in.[1]

A world filled with people who lived for the weekend and spent their paychecks on a new outfit for the club and some alcohol and drugs to go with it.

Miles was only in his teens, but he fell into their world, nonetheless. He played to drunken people, while becoming one of them. Eventually his drinking would lead him into a world of depression, drugs, suicide attempts, and prison.

Miles was born in Tennessee. His mother was a good woman, but his stepfather left much to be desired. His stepfather was a raging, nasty alcoholic who was verbally and physically abusive to Miles. Eventually, when Miles was thirteen, his mother sent him to live with an aunt in Chicago. In reality, she made a choice between her new husband and her son, and her new husband won. Miles still remembers it as the very first time he was rejected by a woman. There were more rejections to come, causing Miles to sink into a life of depression and despair. Miles would choose to self-medicate with drugs.

Miles's cousin introduced him to marijuana as a teen. He did not like the way it made him feel. At the age of twenty-four, the same cousin introduced Miles to cocaine, and he liked it.

They say misery loves company, and Miles's cousin seemed bent on involving Miles with drugs.

By this time, Miles was playing in a band that was gaining some recognition. They were presented with an offer to tour in Japan for a year. After serious consideration by the band members, they decided not to do it.

"I was so extremely disappointed by the fact that we weren't going to take advantage of such an exciting offer. But, I was not the one who owned the equipment or had the money, so I was powerless in the decision. In retrospect, I can understand why they didn't want to go . . . the other band members had families and craved security rather than adventure at that point."

Still, Miles sank into a very serious depression at the idea of losing what he perceived to be

MYTH		FACT
Teenagers and children are too young to get addicted.	VS.	Addiction can occur at any age. Even unborn babies can get addicted because of their mother's drug use.[2]

a great opportunity. He sank deeper into his cocaine addiction. "My band members didn't trust me around the equipment, they couldn't depend on me at all. I don't blame them—at the time it was very hurtful to me, but looking back on the situation, I wouldn't have trusted me either. I was capable of doing anything, including stealing from them, to get money for my next fix." Eventually his band broke up.

Miles had to find a way to make money, and so a natural choice for him was to sell cocaine. He began making sales on the street. He would hold ten to twenty plastic bags filled with cocaine in the bottom of his mouth along his lower jaw line. He learned to talk with the bags in his mouth so that no one would know what he was hiding in there. And if, by chance, a police officer approached, he could always just swallow the bags to hide the evidence. His lower jaw line was always numb from the cocaine seeping into his bloodstream through the bags.

One night, when Miles was making a cocaine drop-off, he walked in on his customers freebasing, and was invited to try. Even though he enjoyed it, it was not until he was introduced to crack that his life spiraled out of control toward death.

Think About It³ . . .

- **Cocaine, in any form, is illegal.**

- **Even first-time cocaine users can have seizures or fatal heart attacks.**

- **Combining cocaine with other drugs or alcohol is extremely dangerous. The effects of one drug can magnify the effects of another, and mixing substances can be deadly.**

- **Cocaine impairs judgment, which may lead to unwise decisions about sexual activity. This can increase risk for HIV/AIDS, other diseases, rape, and unplanned pregnancy.**

- **The vast majority of teens are not using cocaine. According to a 2002 study, less than 1 percent of teens are regular cocaine users. In fact, 97 percent of teens have never even tried cocaine.**

"When I tried crack, it was all over for me. I loved the high, and I was out of it—just disappeared—for weeks. I lost a ton of weight—dropped to a gaunt 160 pounds. None of my clothes fit me. My habit was at about $500 per day . . . money I was getting from stealing and doing things that I never thought I'd do. I became homeless at age 36 or 37, and I just sat on a street corner."

There were many physical and legal repercussions of Miles's drug addiction. At forty years old, he now has dentures—he lost all of his teeth due to the bone and tissue being worn down from the cocaine he used to hide in the bottom of his mouth. He has no nose hair—it was permanently burned from snorting his drugs. "I know I messed up the inside of my nasal passages due to my years of drug use," admitted Miles.

"I was never arrested until the age of twenty-eight, then I was arrested once a year, like clockwork, thereafter. Usually on some stupid charge—but always related either directly or indirectly to drugs. Either it was for knocking over a gas station or driving on a suspended license or property damage."

The turning point of Miles's life came when he

was in jail for sixty days in 2001. He was forced through withdrawal, and had what he describes as a "spiritual encounter." One night, he began throwing up and sweating, and he denounced all of the sin in his life. When he left jail he was completely clean and searching for a recovery program that would help him to remain drug free. He entered Alcoholics Anonymous and found that he could not personally connect with the concepts of the program. He moved on to Narcotics Anonymous, which he identified with a bit more, but he still knew it was not for him. His aunt and uncle eventually gave him an application for Teen Challenge. In fact, it was the same application he had used as a mat for chopping up his drugs a few years before.

Miles reflected on his life and his family and admits that even though they did "nothing but love him—even through tough love," they were also horribly ashamed and embarrassed of him and his drug use. "The truth is that many people in my family were moving forward, getting college degrees, entering the corporate workforce and starting families."

Miles was accepted into the program and

Users may do anything for their next fix, including hiding drugs in school or in their school bags.

moved to the desert Southwest. The program was about a year in length.

"When I left the program, I felt as though I 'deserved' all of the things in life that I hadn't had but wanted . . . a high-paying job, a family, a home. When those things didn't come instantly to me, I was disappointed. Soon after leaving the program, I fell off the wagon for about thirty days—I started going to strip clubs, doing drugs. Luckily, I had kept in touch with the program director during the months that I had left the program, and he was praying for me the entire time. He invited me back to the program, and I've been clean ever since."

Miles moved up from a program student to a staff assistant and will soon be a full staff member. He visits high schools on a regular basis, along with other program participants, to share his story. Miles still has dreams of a family and a home, but he believes that these things will happen in due time.

Reflecting on his years as an addict, Miles summarizes, "I wanted the adventure . . . but it costs people everything they have. If you want a wounded soul and a sick spirit, then do drugs. Drugs will take you to places you don't want to go and introduce you to people you don't want to meet. When you try drugs, you are opening doors that are hard to close."

CHAPTER SIX

AGAINST ALL ODDS

Miles did not have a difficult time finding a program that was right for him, but he had to want to recover. He had already been through the sickening, dizzying effects of physical withdrawal from cocaine and crack: vomiting, night sweats, hallucinations, and fever. Now, it was time for his spirit to recover.

Miles had been searching for internal peace for a long time. He was raised a Baptist but had studied the beliefs of Islam and numerous other faiths. He found a program that is Christian-based, but that accepts addicts from any denomination.

Teen Challenge was established in 1958 by David Wilkerson and has since grown to more than 170 centers in the United States and 250 centers worldwide.[1]

Teen Challenge goes to schools around the world and educates teens about the dangers of drugs. Teen Challenge reaches out to people in juvenile halls, jails, and prisons. Their centers hold weekly support group meetings, and hold classes during the week for the program members.[2]

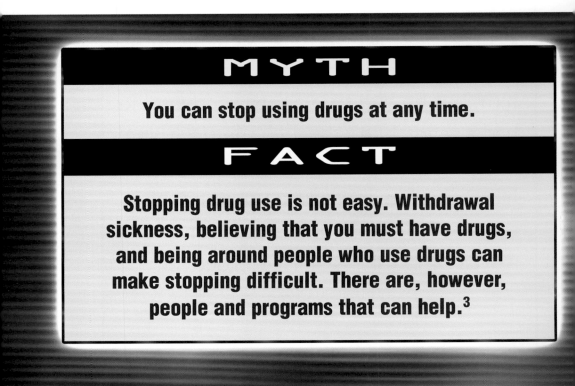

MYTH

You can stop using drugs at any time.

FACT

Stopping drug use is not easy. Withdrawal sickness, believing that you must have drugs, and being around people who use drugs can make stopping difficult. There are, however, people and programs that can help.[3]

The program lasts one year. Program members live at the centers and learn how to live drug-free lives. During that year, they do not hold outside jobs, and all of their attention is focused on the program. Residents follow strict rules and discipline. All residents follow a daily schedule, which includes chapel, Bible classes, and work assignments on or near the grounds.[4]

Miles found the program that worked well for him and has now been clean for eighteen months. He knows that it is a long, hard road and that he needs to be vigilant in his constant fight against drugs. He also knows now that he is not entitled to anything, although he is very hopeful about someday achieving his goals.

"One of my greatest pieces of advice to young people, whether drug users or not, is to learn how to endure pain. Pain is a motivator; it shouldn't be a stumbling block. When trials come, I try to navigate through it, not necessarily around it. As an American society, we are hurting ourselves by not dealing with reality and embracing it—it's life. Life happens," says Miles.[5]

Treatment of cocaine abuse is complex. The user has to have his physical need for cocaine addressed, but also therapists and counselors must address emotional, psychological, or mental problems that may have existed before and during the addict's drug use. Many addicts, like Miles, turn to drugs, such as crack or cocaine, in order to self-medicate for issues in their lives that are causing them to be depressed. However, instead of fixing their problems, they are adding to them.

Right now, there are no medications available to treat cocaine addiction, although possible medications are being researched aggressively. Antidepressant drugs have been shown to be of some benefit if an addict had mood changes resulting from withdrawal. Medications are also currently being developed to deal with the acute emergencies, such as stroke and cardiac arrest, resulting from excessive cocaine abuse.

A number of behavioral treatments have been found to be effective for cocaine addiction, including both residential and outpatient approaches using psychological and psychiatric consultation, motivation enhancement, and relapse prevention. Behavioral treatment is often the only available treatment. However, researchers know that the ideal method of treatment would be a combined approach of medicine and behavioral intervention.

Spot the Signs[b] . . .

How can you tell if a friend is using cocaine? Sometimes it is tough to tell. But there are signs you can look for if you suspect something may not be right. If your friend has one or more of the following signs, he or she may be using cocaine or other illegal drugs.

- Red, bloodshot eyes
- A runny nose or frequent sniffing
- A change in groups of friends
- Acting withdrawn, depressed, tired, or careless about personal appearance
- Losing interest in school, family, or activities he or she used to enjoy
- Frequently needing money

What can you do to help someone who is using cocaine?

Be a real friend. Save his or her life. Encourage your friend to stop or seek professional help.

Quotes on Cocaine

"I wouldn't take them because they could make a hole in your throat and you could die."[7]

"I was and am too scared to put something like that in my body . . . too afraid of the repercussions."[8]

"When you start fooling around with something like cocaine . . . something that messes with your mind and that you may become addicted to, that's heavy duty."[9]

"I OD'd and it scared me enough to stay away. I have been clean for fourteen months, and never looked back."[10]

A patient's personality and specific needs must be taken into account when choosing a program of behavioral intervention. There are a few different types of programs available, each with a different approach to intervention. Because of the seriousness of cocaine or crack addiction and the danger of relapse, the type of program that is chosen for an addict is an extremely important component to the addict's recovery. One-year follow-up interviews with a national sample of 1,605 people treated for cocaine dependence showed that longer treatment stays are related to better outcomes when it comes to kicking the cocaine habit.[11]

It may be tough to know where to turn when you or someone you love is in need of help for his or her addiction, but there is help available. There are many people of all ages and backgrounds who have become addicted to cocaine, even just after the first use. Unlike cocaine addiction, recovery is all under one's control.

GLOSSARY

addiction—Compulsive physiological and psychological need for a habit-forming substance.

alkaloid drug—Any of a number of nitrogen-containing organic substances, usually colorless, crystalline, and bitter, such as caffeine, morphine, quinine, and cocaine, which are known for their medicinal or poisonous attributes.

amphetamine—A central nervous system stimulant that increases energy and decreases appetite; used to treat narcolepsy and some forms of depression.

anesthetic—A drug, gas, etc. used to produce a partial or total loss of sensation and limited to a specific area or involving a loss of consciousness.

antidepressants—A group of drugs used in treating depressive disorders.

archaeologists—People who study ancient cultures.

autopsy—The examination of a dead body, for the purpose of ascertaining the cause of death or nature of a disease; a post-mortem examination.

caffeine—A bitter alkaloid, found in coffee and tea, that is used as a stimulant.

coca—The plant, *Erythroxylon*, from which cocaine is derived. Also refers to the leaves of this plant.

cocaine—A colorless or white crystalline alkaloid, $C_{17}H_{21}NO_4$, extracted from coca leaves, sometimes used in medicine as a local anesthetic, especially for the eyes, nose, or throat; and widely used as an illicit drug for its euphoric and stimulating effects. Also called Toot, Snow, Coke, Flake, and C.

coroner—A public official who investigates any death not due to natural causes.

crack—A form of cocaine that comes in small lumps and makes a crackling sound when heated. Also called "rock."

craving—A powerful, often uncontrollable desire.

DEA—Drug Enforcement Administration.

euphoria—A feeling of great happiness, well-being, or elation.

freebase—A purified solid form of cocaine developed in the 1970s which is not water soluble and must be vaporized and inhaled to be absorbed.

hit—An amount of a drug taken at one time.

injecting—The act of using a needle to release the drug directly into the bloodstream.

intervention—The act or fact of interfering so as to modify, especially to prevent harm or to improve functioning.

narcotic—A drug.

smoking—Involves inhaling the drug vapor or smoke into the lungs where absorption into the bloodstream is as rapid as by injection.

snort—To inhale through the nose.

soundings—Scientific measurements.

street value—The amount of money cocaine would sell for on the streets.

withdrawal—A variety of symptoms that occur after use of an addictive drug is reduced or stopped.

CHAPTER NOTES

Chapter 1. Wild West on Water

1. Tony Perry, "13 Tons of Cocaine Found in Boat Hold," *Los Angeles Times*, May 14, 2001, p. 6.

2. Dave Kopel and Mike Krause, "The Prohibitionist's Burden," *National Review Online*, July 10, 2001, <http://www.nationalreview.com/kopel/kopel071001.shtml> (December 9, 2004).

3. Scott Sutherland, JO1(SW), *Navy Assists Coast Guard, U.S. Customs With Record Maritime Cocaine Seizure*, U.S. Navy, March 2, 2003, <http://www.defenselink.mil/specials/drugawareness/usnnews04a.htm> (November 10, 2004).

4. Ibid.

5. Jeremy Schwartz, "Blanket Radar makes trafficking drugs by air hard in S. Texas," *Corpus Christi Caller-Times*, November 20, 2001, <http://www.caller2.com/specials/trafficking/air.html> (December 9, 2004).

6. Ibid.

7. Sutherland, *Navy Assists Coast Guard, U.S. Customs With Record Maritime Cocaine Seizure.*

8. Personal interview with Raphael, October, 2004.

9. "Cocaine," DrugFacts, n.d., <http://www.whitehousedrugpolicy.gov/drugfact/cocaine> (November 10, 2004).

10. "Pablo Escobar," n.d., <http://www.fact-index.com/p/pa/pablo_escobar.html> (December 9, 2004).

11. Ibid.

12. Steven Casteel, "Narco-Terrorism: International Drug Trafficking and Terrorism—a Dangerous Mix," delivered to the Senate Committee on the Judiciary, May 20, 2003.

Chapter 2. The Legend of Snow White

1. Dominic Streatfeild, *Cocaine: An Unauthorized Biography* (New York: St. Martin's Press, 2001), p. 4.
2. Ibid., p. 8.
3. Ibid.
4. "Altitude Sickness," n.d., <http://www.mothernature.com> (November 9, 2004).
5. "Drugs: Myths and Facts," *TeenZone*, n.d., <http://www.actionhealthinc.org/teenzone/articles/article09.htm> (December 9, 2004).
6. "Powder Cocaine," n.d., <http://www.addictions.org> (November 9, 2004).
7. Ibid.
8. Lester Grinspoon and James B. Bakalar, "Medical Uses of Illicit Drugs," *Schaffer Library of Drug Policy*, n.d., <http://www.druglibrary.org/schaffer/hemp/medical/meduse.html> (December 9, 2004).
9. William J. Bailey, "FactLine on Cocaine," January 11, 2004, <http://www.iprc.indiana.edu> (November 11, 2004).
10. Norman S. Miller, Mark S. Gold, and Robert L. Millman, "Cocaine," *American Family Physician*, Volume 39, February 1989, pp. 115–116.
11. "From Coca-Cola to Crack: A History of Cocaine

in the U.S.," 2003, <http://www.cocaineabuse.net/cocaine_crack.html> (November 10, 2004).

Chapter 3. The Legend of the Leaf

1. Dominic Streatfeild, *Cocaine: An Unauthorized Biography* (New York: St. Martin's Press, 2001), p. 4.

2. "Drugs: Myths and Facts," *TeenZone*, n.d., <http://www.actionhealthinc.org/teenzone/articles/article09.htm> (December 9, 2004).

3. Chris Sherman, "Unraveling the Mysteries," *Empires of Mystery*, n.d., <http://sptimes.com/peru/unraveling/html> (December 13, 2004).

4. Amy Miller, "The Inca Empire Of The Sun," *Junior Scholastic*, volume 102, September 6, 1999, p. 22.

5. "Moments of Truth," *Check Yourself: A Place for Teens to Check Where They Are With Drugs and Alcohol*, February 27, 2003, <http://www.checkyourself.com/Moments.aspx?forumid=2&messageid=2&p=57> (December 9, 2004).

6. Teofilo Caso, "Coca protesters turned back from Machu Picchu ruins with warning not to anger mountain gods," Associated Press, *Healthcare CustomWire*, September 30, 2004, <http://listas.rcp.net.pe/pipermail/noticias/2004-September/008179.html> (December 9, 2004).

7. Ibid.

8. "In Search of the Big Bang," n.d., <http://www.cocaine.org> (November 13, 2004).

9. Kevin McCauley, "The Harrison Narcotic Act," 2003,

<http://www.addictiondoctor.com/LibraryPDFs/HarrisonAct.pdf> (December 9, 2004).

10. Elaine Casey, "History of Drug Use and Drug Users in the United States," *Schaffer Library of Drug Policy*, n.d., <http://www.druglibrary.org/schaffer/History/CASEY1.htm> (December 9, 2004).

11. Edward M. Brecher, "The Consumers Union Report on Licit and Illicit Drugs," *Schaffer Library of Drug Policy*, n.d., <http://www.druglibrary.org/schaffer/Library/studies/cu/cumenu.htm> (December 9, 2004).

12. "The Nixon-Presley Meeting," *The National Security Archive, George Washington University*, n.d., <http://www2.gwu.edu/~nsarchiv/nsa/elvis/elnix.html> (December 9, 2004).

13. "Just Say No: Mrs. Reagan's Crusade," n.d., <http://www.reaganlibrary.com/reagan/nancy/just_say_no.asp> (December 9, 2004).

14. Renee Moilanen, "Just Say No Again," January 2004, <http://www.reason.com/0401/fe.rm.just.shtml> (December 9, 2004).

15. Daniel Forbes, "Prime-time Propaganda, " January 13, 2000, <http://dir.salon.com/news.feature/2000/01/13/drugs/index.html?sid=562701> (December 13, 2004).

16. Ibid.

17. "DEA Mission Statement," n.d., <http://www.usdoj.gov/dea/agency/mission.htm> (December 9, 2004).

18. "Operation Blast Furnace," *DEA History Book*, 1985–1990, n.d., <http://www.usdoj.gov/dea/pubs/history/deahistory_04.htm> (December 9, 2004).

19. Ibid.

20. Personal interivew with Raphael, October 2004.

21. "Operation Blast Furnace," *DEA History Book*, 1985–1990, n.d., <http://www.usdoj.gov/dea/pubs/history/deahistory_04.htm> (December 9, 2004).

Chapter 4. The Price to Play

1. Narconon, "Cocaine Addiction information," n.d., <http://www.stopaddiction.com/cocaine_addiction.html> (December 9, 2004).

2. Ibid.

3. National Department of Health and Human Services and SAMHSA's National Clearinghouse for Alcohol and Drug Information, n.d., <http://www.health.org> (November 10, 2004).

4. Personal interview with teen, 2004.

5. "Drugs in Hollywood," n.d., <http://www.eonline.com/Features/Specials/Underbelly/One/index2.html> (December 9, 2004).

6. Ibid.

7. Ibid.

8. Ibid.

9. Ibid.

10. Thomas Carney, "Celebrity fame fatal—suicide of actor David Strickland," *Los Angeles Magazine*, n.d., <http://www.findarticles.com/p/articles/mi_m1346/is_9_44/ai_55588141> (December 9, 2004).

11. "River Phoenix," n.d., <http://en.wikipedia.org/wiki/River_Phoenix> (December 9, 2004).

12. Ibid.

13. "Chris Farley," n.d., <http://www.encyclopedia. thefreedictionary.com/Chris+Farley> (November 16, 2004).

14. Ibid.

15. "Crack Cocaine," n.d., <http://www.usnodrugs. com/crack-cocaine.htm> (December 9, 2004).

16. Ibid.

17. "Drugs: Myths and Facts," *TeenZone*, n.d., <http:// www.actionhealthinc.org/teenzone/articles/ article09.htm> (December 9, 2004).

18. Personal interview with Captain David Campbell, November 2004.

19. "The 'Body Packer Syndrome'—Toxicity Following Ingestion of Illicit Drugs Packaged for Transportation," *Journal of Forensic Sciences*, July 1981, <http://journalsip.astm.org/JOURNAL/FORENSIC/ PAGES/56.htm> (December 9, 2004).

Chapter 5. Time to Face the Music

1. Personal interview with Miles, November 19, 2004.

2. "Drugs: Myths and Facts," *TeenZone*, n.d., <http:// www.actionhealthinc.org/teenzone/articles/ article09.htm> (December 9, 2004).

3. U.S. Department of Health and Human Services, "Tips for Teens: The Truth about Cocaine," n.d., <http://www.health.org/govpubs/phd640i/> (December 9, 2004).

Chapter 6. Against All Odds

1. "About Us," *Teen Challenge*, n.d., <http://www.

teenchallenge.com/index.cfm?infoID=1&centerID= 1194> (December 9, 2004).

2. "About Us," *Teen Challenge*, n.d., <http://www. teenchallenge.com/index.cfm?infoID=1&centerID= 1194> (December 9, 2004).

3. "Drugs: Myths and Facts," *TeenZone*, n.d., <http:// www.actionhealthinc.org/teenzone/articles/ article09.htm> (December 9, 2004).

4. Ibid.

5. Personal interview with Miles, November 19, 2004.

6. U.S. Department of Health and Human Services, "Tips for Teens: The Truth about Cocaine," n.d., <http://www.health.org/govpubs/phd640i/> (December 9, 2004).

7. Personal interview (female, age 12), November 2004.

8. Personal interview (female, age 12), November 2004.

9. Personal interview (male, age 27), November 2004.

10. "Moments of Truth," *Check Yourself: A Place for Teens to Check Where They Are With Drugs and Alcohol*, February 27, 2003, <http://wwwcheckyourself. com/Moments.aspx?forumid=2&messageid=2&p= 57> (December 9, 2004).

11. D. D. Simpson, G. W. Joe, B. W. Fletcher, R. L. Hubbard, and M. D. Anglin, "A National Evaluation of Treatment Outcomes for Cocaine Dependence," *Archives of General Psychiatry*, 56, pp. 506–514.

FURTHER READING

Aretha, David. *Cocaine and Crack.* Berkeley Heights, N.J.: MyReportLinks.com Book, 2005.

Bayer, Linda. *Crack & Cocaine.* Philadelphia, Penn.: Chelsea House Publishers, 2000.

Eller, T. Suzanne. *Real Teens, Real Stories, Real Life.* RiverOak Publishing, 2002.

Gelletly, LeeAnne. *Bolivia.* Philadelphia, Penn.: Mason Crest Publishers, 2004. (This book contains facts about the South American country.)

Hyde, Margaret O. and John F. Setaro. *Drugs 101: An Overview for Teens.* Brookfield, Conn.: Twenty-First Century Books, 2003.

Jacobs, Thomas A. *They Broke the Law, You Be the Judge: True Cases of Teen Crime.* Minneapolis, Minn.: Free Spirit Pub., 2003.

Kuhn, Cynthia, Scott Swartzwelder, and Wilkie Wilson. *Buzzed: The Straight Facts About the Most Used and Abused Drugs From Alcohol to Ecstasy.* New York: W. W. Norton, 2003.

Lennard-Brown, Sarah. *Cocaine.* Chicago: Raintree, 2005.

Wagner, Heather Lehr. *Cocaine.* Philadelphia, Penn.: Chelsea House Publishers, 2003.

INTERNET ADDRESSES

Check Yourself: A Place for Teens to Check
  Where They Are With Drugs and Alcohol
  <http://www.checkyourself.com/>
  *Read other teens' views on drugs and
  alcohol, and read about what they have
  gone through.*

Neuroscience for Kids—Cocaine
  <http://faculty.washington.edu/chudler/coca.
    html>
  Learn more about the effects of cocaine.

Tips for Teens: The Truth About Cocaine
  <http://www.health.org/govpubs/phd640i>
  *Get quick answers to questions about
  cocaine.*

INDEX